Teacher Planner

· ·

WEEKLY & MONTHLY LESSON PLAN

NAME: _____

CLASSROOM: _____

EMAIL: _____

PHONE: _____

EMMELINE & BLOOM

Year at a Glance

AUGUST 2020

S	M	T	W	T	F	S
						1
2	3	4	5	6	7	8
9	10	11	12	13	14	15
16	17	18	19	20	21	22
23	24	25	26	27	28	29
30	31					

SEPTEMBER 2020

S	M	T	W	T	F	S
		1	2	3	4	5
6	7	8	9	10	11	12
13	14	15	16	17	18	19
20	21	22	23	24	25	26
27	28	29	30			

OCTOBER 2020

S	M	T	W	T	F	S
				1	2	3
4	5	6	7	8	9	10
11	12	13	14	15	16	17
18	19	20	21	22	23	24
25	26	27	28	29	30	31

NOVEMBER 2020

S	M	T	W	T	F	S
1	2	3	4	5	6	7
8	9	10	11	12	13	14
15	16	17	18	19	20	21
22	23	24	25	26	27	28
29	30					

DECEMBER 2020

S	M	T	W	T	F	S
		1	2	3	4	5
6	7	8	9	10	11	12
13	14	15	16	17	18	19
20	21	22	23	24	25	26
27	28	29	30	31		

JANUARY 2021

S	M	T	W	T	F	S
					1	2
3	4	5	6	7	8	9
10	11	12	13	14	15	16
17	18	19	20	21	22	23
24	25	26	27	28	29	30
31						

FEBRUARY 2021

S	M	T	W	T	F	S
	1	2	3	4	5	6
7	8	9	10	11	12	13
14	15	16	17	18	19	20
21	22	23	24	25	26	27
28						

MARCH 2021

S	M	T	W	T	F	S
	1	2	3	4	5	6
7	8	9	10	11	12	13
14	15	16	17	18	19	20
21	22	23	24	25	26	27
28	29	30	31			

APRIL 2021

S	M	T	W	T	F	S
				1	2	3
4	5	6	7	8	9	10
11	12	13	14	15	16	17
18	19	20	21	22	23	24
25	26	27	28	29	30	

MAY 2021

S	M	T	W	T	F	S
						1
2	3	4	5	6	7	8
9	10	11	12	13	14	15
16	17	18	19	20	21	22
23	24	25	26	27	28	29
30	31					

JUNE 2021

S	M	T	W	T	F	S
		1	2	3	4	5
6	7	8	9	10	11	12
13	14	15	16	17	18	19
20	21	22	23	24	25	26
27	28	29	30			

JULY 2021

S	M	T	W	T	F	S
				1	2	3
4	5	6	7	8	9	10
11	12	13	14	15	16	17
18	19	20	21	22	23	24
25	26	27	28	29	30	31

Notes

Important Dates

AUGUST

_____ _____
_____ _____
_____ _____
_____ _____
_____ _____
_____ _____
_____ _____

SEPTEMBER

_____ _____
_____ _____
_____ _____
_____ _____
_____ _____
_____ _____
_____ _____

OCTOBER

_____ _____
_____ _____
_____ _____
_____ _____
_____ _____
_____ _____
_____ _____

NOVEMBER

_____ _____
_____ _____
_____ _____
_____ _____
_____ _____
_____ _____
_____ _____

DECEMBER

_____ _____
_____ _____
_____ _____
_____ _____
_____ _____
_____ _____
_____ _____

JANUARY

_____ _____
_____ _____
_____ _____
_____ _____
_____ _____
_____ _____
_____ _____

FEBRUARY

_____ _____
_____ _____
_____ _____
_____ _____
_____ _____
_____ _____

MARCH

_____ _____
_____ _____
_____ _____
_____ _____
_____ _____
_____ _____

APRIL

_____ _____
_____ _____
_____ _____
_____ _____
_____ _____
_____ _____

MAY

_____ _____
_____ _____
_____ _____
_____ _____
_____ _____

JUNE

_____ _____
_____ _____
_____ _____
_____ _____
_____ _____

JULY

_____ _____
_____ _____
_____ _____
_____ _____
_____ _____

Birthdays

AUGUST

_____ _____
_____ _____
_____ _____
_____ _____
_____ _____
_____ _____
_____ _____

SEPTEMBER

_____ _____
_____ _____
_____ _____
_____ _____
_____ _____
_____ _____
_____ _____

OCTOBER

_____ _____
_____ _____
_____ _____
_____ _____
_____ _____
_____ _____
_____ _____

NOVEMBER

_____ _____
_____ _____
_____ _____
_____ _____
_____ _____
_____ _____
_____ _____

DECEMBER

_____ _____
_____ _____
_____ _____
_____ _____
_____ _____
_____ _____
_____ _____

JANUARY

_____ _____
_____ _____
_____ _____
_____ _____
_____ _____
_____ _____
_____ _____

FEBRUARY

_____ _____
_____ _____
_____ _____
_____ _____
_____ _____
_____ _____
_____ _____

MARCH

_____ _____
_____ _____
_____ _____
_____ _____
_____ _____
_____ _____
_____ _____

APRIL

_____ _____
_____ _____
_____ _____
_____ _____
_____ _____
_____ _____
_____ _____

MAY

_____ _____
_____ _____
_____ _____
_____ _____
_____ _____
_____ _____
_____ _____

JUNE

_____ _____
_____ _____
_____ _____
_____ _____
_____ _____
_____ _____
_____ _____

JULY

_____ _____
_____ _____
_____ _____
_____ _____
_____ _____
_____ _____
_____ _____

Class List

FIRST NAME	LAST NAME	NOTES/COMMENTS

Notes

SUNDAY	MONDAY	TUESDAY
26	27	28
02	03	04
09	10	11
16	17	18
23	24	25
30	31	

AUGUST BANK HOLIDAY (UK)

August 2020

WEDNESDAY	THURSDAY	FRIDAY	SATURDAY
29	30	31	01
05	06	07	08
12	13	14	15
19	20	21	22
26	27	28	29

July 27 - August 2, 2020

SUBJECT	MONDAY	27	TUESDAY	28	WEDNESDAY	29

THURSDAY	30	FRIDAY	31	SATURDAY	01

SUNDAY 02

GOALS

- ◯
- ◯
- ◯
- ◯
- ◯
- ◯
- ◯
- ◯

NOTES

August 3 - August 9, 2020

SUBJECT	MONDAY	03	TUESDAY	04	WEDNESDAY	05

Words of Wisdom:

THURSDAY	06	FRIDAY	07	SATURDAY	08

SUNDAY | 09

GOALS

- ◯
- ◯
- ◯
- ◯
- ◯
- ◯
- ◯
- ◯

NOTES

August 10 - August 16, 2020

SUBJECT	MONDAY	10	TUESDAY	11	WEDNESDAY	12

THURSDAY	13	FRIDAY	14	SATURDAY	15

SUNDAY	16

GOALS

- ○
- ○
- ○
- ○
- ○
- ○
- ○
- ○

NOTES

August 17 - August 23, 2020

SUBJECT	MONDAY	17	TUESDAY	18	WEDNESDAY	19

THURSDAY	20	FRIDAY	21	SATURDAY	22

SUNDAY	23

GOALS

- ◯
- ◯
- ◯
- ◯
- ◯
- ◯
- ◯
- ◯

NOTES

August 24 - August 30, 2020

SUBJECT	MONDAY	24	TUESDAY	25	WEDNESDAY	26

THURSDAY	27	FRIDAY	28	SATURDAY	29

SUNDAY	30

GOALS

○
○
○
○
○
○
○
○

NOTES

Notes

_____

_____

_____

_____

_____

_____

_____

_____

_____

_____

_____

_____

_____

_____

_____

_____

_____

_____

_____

_____

_____

_____

_____

SUNDAY	MONDAY	TUESDAY
30	31	01
06	07	08
	LABOR/LABOUR DAY (US/CAN)	
13	14	15
20	21	22
		FIRST DAY OF AUTUMN
27	28	29

September 2020

WEDNESDAY	THURSDAY	FRIDAY	SATURDAY
02	03	04	05
09	10	11	12
		PATRIOT DAY (US)	
16	17	18	19
23	24	25	26
30	01	02	03

August 31 - September 6, 2020

SUBJECT	MONDAY	31	TUESDAY	01	WEDNESDAY	02

THURSDAY	03	FRIDAY	04	SATURDAY	05

SUNDAY | 06

GOALS

- ◯
- ◯
- ◯
- ◯
- ◯
- ◯
- ◯
- ◯

NOTES

September 7 - September 13, 2020

SUBJECT	MONDAY	07	TUESDAY	08	WEDNESDAY	09

THURSDAY	10	FRIDAY	11	SATURDAY	12

SUNDAY 13

GOALS

- ○
- ○
- ○
- ○
- ○
- ○
- ○
- ○

NOTES

September 14 - September 20, 2020

SUBJECT	MONDAY	14	TUESDAY	15	WEDNESDAY	16

THURSDAY	17	FRIDAY	18	SATURDAY	19

SUNDAY	20

GOALS

- ○
- ○
- ○
- ○
- ○
- ○
- ○
- ○

NOTES

September 21 - September 27, 2020

SUBJECT	MONDAY	21	TUESDAY	22	WEDNESDAY	23

MY STUDENTS DESERVE MY BEST.

THURSDAY	24	FRIDAY	25	SATURDAY	26

SUNDAY | 27

GOALS

- ◯
- ◯
- ◯
- ◯
- ◯
- ◯
- ◯
- ◯

NOTES

Notes

_____
_____
_____
_____
_____
_____
_____
_____
_____
_____
_____
_____
_____
_____
_____
_____
_____
_____
_____
_____
_____
_____

SUNDAY	MONDAY	TUESDAY
27	28	29
04	05	06
11	12	13
	COLUMBUS DAY (US) THANKSGIVING (CAN)	
18	19	20
25	26	27

October 2020

WEDNESDAY	THURSDAY	FRIDAY	SATURDAY
30	01	02	03
07	08	09	10
14	15	16	17
21	22	23	24
28	29	30	31 HALLOWEEN

September 28 - October 4, 2020

SUBJECT	MONDAY	28	TUESDAY	29	WEDNESDAY	30

THURSDAY	01	FRIDAY	02	SATURDAY	03

SUNDAY 04

GOALS

- ◯
- ◯
- ◯
- ◯
- ◯
- ◯
- ◯
- ◯

NOTES

October 5 - October 11, 2020

SUBJECT	MONDAY	05	TUESDAY	06	WEDNESDAY	07

THURSDAY	08	FRIDAY	09	SATURDAY	10

SUNDAY | 11

GOALS

- ◯
- ◯
- ◯
- ◯
- ◯
- ◯
- ◯
- ◯

NOTES

October 12 - October 18, 2020

SUBJECT	MONDAY	12	TUESDAY	13	WEDNESDAY	14

THURSDAY	15	FRIDAY	16	SATURDAY	17

SUNDAY	18

GOALS

○
○
○
○
○
○
○
○

NOTES

October 19 - October 25, 2020

SUBJECT	MONDAY	19	TUESDAY	20	WEDNESDAY	21

Words of Wisdom: I BELIEVE IN EACH OF MY STUDENTS.

THURSDAY	22	FRIDAY	23	SATURDAY	24

SUNDAY | 25

GOALS

- ○
- ○
- ○
- ○
- ○
- ○
- ○
- ○

NOTES

October 26 - November 1, 2020

SUBJECT	MONDAY	26	TUESDAY	27	WEDNESDAY	28

THURSDAY	29	FRIDAY	30	SATURDAY	31

SUNDAY	01

GOALS

- ◯
- ◯
- ◯
- ◯
- ◯
- ◯
- ◯
- ◯

NOTES

Notes

SUNDAY	MONDAY	TUESDAY
01	02	03
DAYLIGHT SAVING TIME ENDS		
08	09	10
15	16	17
22	23	24
29	30	01

November 2020

WEDNESDAY	THURSDAY	FRIDAY	SATURDAY
04	05	06	07
11	12	13	14
VETERAN'S DAY (US) REMEMBRANCE DAY (CAN)			
18	19	20	21
25	26	27	28
	THANKSGIVING (US)		
02	03	04	05

November 2 - November 8, 2020

SUBJECT	MONDAY	02	TUESDAY	03	WEDNESDAY	04

THURSDAY	05	FRIDAY	06	SATURDAY	07

SUNDAY | 08

GOALS

- ◯
- ◯
- ◯
- ◯
- ◯
- ◯
- ◯
- ◯

NOTES

November 9 - November 15, 2020

SUBJECT	MONDAY	09	TUESDAY	10	WEDNESDAY	11

THURSDAY	12	FRIDAY	13	SATURDAY	14

SUNDAY	15

GOALS

- ◯
- ◯
- ◯
- ◯
- ◯
- ◯
- ◯
- ◯

NOTES

November 16 - November 22, 2020

SUBJECT	MONDAY	16	TUESDAY	17	WEDNESDAY	18

THURSDAY	19	FRIDAY	20	SATURDAY	21

SUNDAY	22

GOALS

- ○
- ○
- ○
- ○
- ○
- ○
- ○
- ○

NOTES

November 23 - November 29, 2020

SUBJECT	MONDAY	23	TUESDAY	24	WEDNESDAY	25

I WILL TEACH MY STUDENTS TO COUNT
BUT MORE IMPORTANTLY WHAT COUNTS.

THURSDAY	26	FRIDAY	27	SATURDAY	28

SUNDAY | 29

GOALS

- ◯
- ◯
- ◯
- ◯
- ◯
- ◯
- ◯
- ◯

NOTES

Notes

SUNDAY	MONDAY	TUESDAY
29	30	01
06	07	08
13	14	15
20	21	22
	FIRST DAY OF WINTER	
27	28	29

_____
_____
_____
_____
_____
_____
_____
_____
_____
_____
_____
_____
_____
_____
_____
_____
_____
_____
_____
_____
_____

December 2020

WEDNESDAY	THURSDAY	FRIDAY	SATURDAY
02	03	04	05
09	10	11	12
16	17	18	19
23	24 CHRISTMAS EVE	25 CHRISTMAS	26 BOXING DAY (CAN/UK)
30	31 NEW YEAR'S EVE	01	02

November 30 - December 6, 2020

SUBJECT	MONDAY	30	TUESDAY	01	WEDNESDAY	02

THURSDAY	03	FRIDAY	04	SATURDAY	05

SUNDAY 06

GOALS

- ◯
- ◯
- ◯
- ◯
- ◯
- ◯
- ◯
- ◯

NOTES

December 7 - December 13, 2020

SUBJECT	MONDAY	07	TUESDAY	08	WEDNESDAY	09

THURSDAY	10	FRIDAY	11	SATURDAY	12

SUNDAY	13

GOALS

- ◯
- ◯
- ◯
- ◯
- ◯
- ◯
- ◯
- ◯

NOTES

December 14 - December 20, 2020

SUBJECT	MONDAY	14	TUESDAY	15	WEDNESDAY	16

THURSDAY	17	FRIDAY	18	SATURDAY	19

SUNDAY 20

GOALS

- ○
- ○
- ○
- ○
- ○
- ○
- ○
- ○

NOTES

December 21 - December 27, 2020

SUBJECT	MONDAY	21	TUESDAY	22	WEDNESDAY	23

Words of Wisdom:

THURSDAY	24	FRIDAY	25	SATURDAY	26

SUNDAY 27

GOALS

- ◯
- ◯
- ◯
- ◯
- ◯
- ◯
- ◯
- ◯

NOTES

Notes

_____

_____

_____

_____

_____

_____

_____

_____

_____

_____

_____

_____

_____

_____

_____

_____

_____

_____

_____

_____

_____

_____

_____

SUNDAY	MONDAY	TUESDAY
27	28	29
03	04	05
10	11	12
17	18	19
	MARTIN LUTHER KING JR. DAY (US)	
24	25	26
31		

January 2021

WEDNESDAY	THURSDAY	FRIDAY	SATURDAY
30	31	01 NEW YEAR'S DAY	02
06	07	08	09
13	14	15	16
20	21	22	23
27	28	29	30

December 28, 2020 - January 3, 2021

SUBJECT	MONDAY	28	TUESDAY	29	WEDNESDAY	30

THURSDAY	31	FRIDAY	01	SATURDAY	02

SUNDAY 03

GOALS

- ○
- ○
- ○
- ○
- ○
- ○
- ○
- ○

NOTES

January 4 - January 10, 2020

SUBJECT	MONDAY	04	TUESDAY	05	WEDNESDAY	06

Words of Wisdom:

I WILL RESPOND CALMLY AND PATIENTLY TO EVERYTHING
THAT HAPPENS TODAY.

THURSDAY	07	FRIDAY	08	SATURDAY	09

SUNDAY 10

GOALS

- ◯
- ◯
- ◯
- ◯
- ◯
- ◯
- ◯
- ◯

NOTES

January 11 - January 17, 2021

SUBJECT	MONDAY	11	TUESDAY	12	WEDNESDAY	13

I HAVE THE ABILITY TO CHANGE MY STUDENT'S LIVES,
I WON'T WASTE IT.

THURSDAY	14	FRIDAY	15	SATURDAY	16

SUNDAY	17

GOALS

- ◯
- ◯
- ◯
- ◯
- ◯
- ◯
- ◯
- ◯

NOTES

January 18 - January 24, 2021

SUBJECT	MONDAY	18	TUESDAY	19	WEDNESDAY	20

Words of Wisdom:

TEACHERS ARE THE ONLY ONES WHO LOSE SLEEP OVER OTHER PEOPLE'S CHILDREN.

THURSDAY	21	FRIDAY	22	SATURDAY	23

SUNDAY	24

GOALS

- ◯
- ◯
- ◯
- ◯
- ◯
- ◯
- ◯
- ◯

NOTES

January 25 - January 31, 2021

SUBJECT	MONDAY	25	TUESDAY	26	WEDNESDAY	27

THURSDAY	28	FRIDAY	29	SATURDAY	30

SUNDAY	31

GOALS

- ○
- ○
- ○
- ○
- ○
- ○
- ○
- ○

NOTES

Notes

_____

_____

_____

_____

_____

_____

_____

_____

_____

_____

_____

_____

_____

_____

_____

_____

_____

_____

_____

_____

_____

_____

_____

_____

_____

_____

_____

SUNDAY	MONDAY	TUESDAY
31	01	02
07	08	09
14 VALENTINE'S DAY	15 PRESIDENT'S DAY (US)	16
21	22	23
28	01	02

WEDNESDAY	THURSDAY	FRIDAY	SATURDAY
03	04	05	06
10	11	12	13
17	18	19	20
24	25	26	27
03	04	05	06

february 1 - february 7. 2021

SUBJECT	MONDAY	01	TUESDAY	02	WEDNESDAY	03

THURSDAY	04	FRIDAY	05	SATURDAY	06

SUNDAY | 07

GOALS

- ○
- ○
- ○
- ○
- ○
- ○
- ○
- ○

NOTES

february 8 - february 14, 2021

SUBJECT	MONDAY	08	TUESDAY	09	WEDNESDAY	10

THURSDAY	11	FRIDAY	12	SATURDAY	13

SUNDAY	14

GOALS

- ◯
- ◯
- ◯
- ◯
- ◯
- ◯
- ◯
- ◯

NOTES

february 15 - february 21, 2021

SUBJECT	MONDAY	15	TUESDAY	16	WEDNESDAY	17

THURSDAY	18	FRIDAY	19	SATURDAY	20

SUNDAY 21

GOALS

- ◯
- ◯
- ◯
- ◯
- ◯
- ◯
- ◯
- ◯

NOTES

february 22 - february 28, 2021

SUBJECT	MONDAY	22	TUESDAY	23	WEDNESDAY	24

Words of Wisdom:

THURSDAY	25	FRIDAY	26	SATURDAY	27

SUNDAY	28

GOALS

- ◯
- ◯
- ◯
- ◯
- ◯
- ◯
- ◯
- ◯

NOTES

Notes

SUNDAY	MONDAY	TUESDAY
28	01	02
07	08	09
14	15	16
21	22	23
28	29	30

DAYLIGHT SAVING TIME BEGINS

March 2021

WEDNESDAY	THURSDAY	FRIDAY	SATURDAY
03	04	05	06
10	11	12	13
17	18	19	20
ST. PATRICK'S DAY			FIRST DAY OF SPRING
24	25	26	27
31	01	02	03

March 1 - March 7, 2021

SUBJECT	MONDAY	01	TUESDAY	02	WEDNESDAY	03

THURSDAY	04	FRIDAY	05	SATURDAY	06

SUNDAY	07

GOALS

- ○
- ○
- ○
- ○
- ○
- ○
- ○
- ○

NOTES

March 8 - March 14, 2021

SUBJECT	MONDAY	08	TUESDAY	09	WEDNESDAY	10

THURSDAY	11	FRIDAY	12	SATURDAY	13

SUNDAY 14

GOALS

- ◯
- ◯
- ◯
- ◯
- ◯
- ◯
- ◯
- ◯

NOTES

March 15 - March 21, 2021

SUBJECT	MONDAY	15	TUESDAY	16	WEDNESDAY	17

THURSDAY	18	FRIDAY	19	SATURDAY	20

SUNDAY	21

GOALS

○
○
○
○
○
○
○
○

NOTES

March 22 - March 28, 2021

SUBJECT	MONDAY	22	TUESDAY	23	WEDNESDAY	24

THURSDAY	25	FRIDAY	26	SATURDAY	27

SUNDAY 28

GOALS

- ○
- ○
- ○
- ○
- ○
- ○
- ○
- ○

NOTES

Notes

SUNDAY	MONDAY	TUESDAY
28	29	30
04 EASTER	05 EASTER MONDAY	06
11	12	13
18	19	20
25	26	27

April 2021

WEDNESDAY	THURSDAY	FRIDAY	SATURDAY
31	01	02 GOOD FRIDAY	03
07	08	09	10
14	15	16	17
21	22	23	24
28	29	30	01

March 29 - April 4, 2021

SUBJECT	MONDAY	29	TUESDAY	30	WEDNESDAY	31

TEACHING IS THE GREATEST ACT OF OPTIMISM.
-COLLEEN WILCOX

THURSDAY	01	FRIDAY	02	SATURDAY	03

SUNDAY	04

GOALS

- ○
- ○
- ○
- ○
- ○
- ○
- ○
- ○

NOTES

April 5 – April 11, 2021

SUBJECT	MONDAY	05	TUESDAY	06	WEDNESDAY	07

THURSDAY	08	FRIDAY	09	SATURDAY	10

SUNDAY | 11

GOALS

- ○
- ○
- ○
- ○
- ○
- ○
- ○
- ○

NOTES

April 12 - April 18, 2021

SUBJECT	MONDAY	12	TUESDAY	13	WEDNESDAY	14

Words of Wisdom: EDUCATION BREEDS CONFIDENCE. CONFIDENCE BREEDS HOPE. HOPE BREEDS PEACE. -CONFUCIUS

THURSDAY	15	FRIDAY	16	SATURDAY	17

SUNDAY | 18

GOALS

- ○
- ○
- ○
- ○
- ○
- ○
- ○
- ○

NOTES

April 19 - April 25, 2021

SUBJECT	MONDAY	19	TUESDAY	20	WEDNESDAY	21

THURSDAY	22	FRIDAY	23	SATURDAY	24

SUNDAY | 25

GOALS

- ○
- ○
- ○
- ○
- ○
- ○
- ○
- ○

NOTES

April 26 - May 2, 2021

SUBJECT	MONDAY	26	TUESDAY	27	WEDNESDAY	28

THURSDAY	29	FRIDAY	30	SATURDAY	01

SUNDAY 02

GOALS

- ◯
- ◯
- ◯
- ◯
- ◯
- ◯
- ◯
- ◯

NOTES

Notes

SUNDAY	MONDAY	TUESDAY
25	26	27
02	03 MAY DAY (UK)	04
09 MOTHER'S DAY	10	11
16	17	18
23	24 VICTORIA DAY (CAN)	25
30	31 MEMORIAL DAY (US) SPRING BANK HOLIDAY (UK)	

May 2021

WEDNESDAY	THURSDAY	FRIDAY	SATURDAY
28	29	30	01
05	06	07	08
CINCO DE MAYO			
12	13	14	15
19	20	21	22
26	27	28	29

May 3 - May 9, 2021

SUBJECT	MONDAY	03	TUESDAY	04	WEDNESDAY	05

Words of Wisdom: EVERY DAY MAY NOT BE GOOD BUT THERE IS GOOD IN EVERY DAY.

THURSDAY	06	FRIDAY	07	SATURDAY	08

SUNDAY | 09

GOALS

- ○
- ○
- ○
- ○
- ○
- ○
- ○
- ○

NOTES

May 10 - May 16, 2021

SUBJECT	MONDAY	10	TUESDAY	11	WEDNESDAY	12

THURSDAY	13	FRIDAY	14	SATURDAY	15

SUNDAY	16

GOALS

- ○
- ○
- ○
- ○
- ○
- ○
- ○
- ○

NOTES

May 17 - May 23, 2021

SUBJECT	MONDAY	17	TUESDAY	18	WEDNESDAY	19

THURSDAY	20	FRIDAY	21	SATURDAY	22

SUNDAY 23

GOALS

- ○
- ○
- ○
- ○
- ○
- ○
- ○
- ○

NOTES

May 24 - May 30, 2021

SUBJECT	MONDAY	24	TUESDAY	25	WEDNESDAY	26

THURSDAY	27	FRIDAY	28	SATURDAY	29

SUNDAY | 30

GOALS

- ◯
- ◯
- ◯
- ◯
- ◯
- ◯
- ◯
- ◯

NOTES

Notes

_____
_____
_____
_____
_____
_____
_____
_____
_____
_____
_____
_____
_____
_____
_____
_____
_____
_____
_____
_____
_____
_____
_____
_____

SUNDAY	MONDAY	TUESDAY
30	31	01
06	07	08
13	14	15
20	21	22
FATHER'S DAY FIRST DAY OF SUMMER		
27	28	29

June 2021

WEDNESDAY	THURSDAY	FRIDAY	SATURDAY
02	03	04	05
09	10	11	12
16	17	18	19
23	24	25	26
30	01	02	03

May 31 - June 6, 2021

SUBJECT	MONDAY	31	TUESDAY	01	WEDNESDAY	02

THURSDAY	03	FRIDAY	04	SATURDAY	05

SUNDAY	06

GOALS

- ◯
- ◯
- ◯
- ◯
- ◯
- ◯
- ◯
- ◯

NOTES

June 7 - June 13, 2021

SUBJECT	MONDAY	07	TUESDAY	08	WEDNESDAY	09

I MAKE A DIFFERENCE IN MY STUDENTS' LIVES.
THE WORK I DO MATTERS.

THURSDAY	10	FRIDAY	11	SATURDAY	12

SUNDAY 13

GOALS

○
○
○
○
○
○
○
○

NOTES

June 14 - June 20, 2021

SUBJECT	MONDAY	14	TUESDAY	15	WEDNESDAY	16

I AM A COMPETENT AND CAPABLE TEACHER.
I AM CONFIDENT IN MY ABILITIES.

THURSDAY	17	FRIDAY	18	SATURDAY	19

SUNDAY	20

GOALS

- ○
- ○
- ○
- ○
- ○
- ○
- ○
- ○

NOTES

June 21 - June 27, 2021

SUBJECT	MONDAY	21	TUESDAY	22	WEDNESDAY	23

THURSDAY	24	FRIDAY	25	SATURDAY	26

SUNDAY 27

GOALS

- ○
- ○
- ○
- ○
- ○
- ○
- ○
- ○

NOTES

Notes

SUNDAY	MONDAY	TUESDAY
27	28	29
04	05	06
INDEPENDENCE DAY (US)		
11	12	13
18	19	20
25	26	27

WEDNESDAY	THURSDAY	FRIDAY	SATURDAY
30	01	02	03
	CANADA DAY (CAN)		
07	08	09	10
14	15	16	17
21	22	23	24
28	29	30	31

June 28 - July 4, 2021

SUBJECT	MONDAY	28	TUESDAY	29	WEDNESDAY	30

Words of Wisdom:

EVERY CHILD IS ONE CARING ADULT AWAY
FROM BEING A SUCCESS STORY.

THURSDAY	01	FRIDAY	02	SATURDAY	03

SUNDAY	04

GOALS

- ◯
- ◯
- ◯
- ◯
- ◯
- ◯
- ◯
- ◯

NOTES

July 5 - July 11, 2021

SUBJECT	MONDAY	05	TUESDAY	06	WEDNESDAY	07

THURSDAY	08	FRIDAY	09	SATURDAY	10

SUNDAY	11

GOALS

- ◯
- ◯
- ◯
- ◯
- ◯
- ◯
- ◯
- ◯

NOTES

July 12 - July 18, 2021

SUBJECT	MONDAY	12	TUESDAY	13	WEDNESDAY	14

Words of Wisdom:

THURSDAY	15	FRIDAY	16	SATURDAY	17

SUNDAY 18

GOALS

- ◯
- ◯
- ◯
- ◯
- ◯
- ◯
- ◯
- ◯

NOTES

July 19 - July 25, 2021

SUBJECT	MONDAY	19	TUESDAY	20	WEDNESDAY	21

THURSDAY	22	FRIDAY	23	SATURDAY	24

SUNDAY	25

GOALS

- ◯
- ◯
- ◯
- ◯
- ◯
- ◯
- ◯
- ◯

NOTES

July 26 - August 1, 2021

SUBJECT	MONDAY	26	TUESDAY	27	WEDNESDAY	28

Words of Wisdom:

I AM A BETTER TEACHER BECAUSE OF MY STUDENTS.
MY STUDENTS ARE BETTER PEOPLE BECAUSE OF ME.

THURSDAY	29	FRIDAY	30	SATURDAY	31

SUNDAY 01

GOALS

- ○
- ○
- ○
- ○
- ○
- ○
- ○
- ○

NOTES

Notes

Notes

Notes

Notes

Notes

Notes